The ABC's of Personal Finance Workbook

by

Debbi King

Copyright © 2012 by Debbi King

The ABC's of Personal Finance Workbook
by Debbi King

Printed in the United States of America

ISBN 9781480120648

All rights reserved solely by the author. The author guarantees all contents are original and do not infringe upon the legal rights of any other person or work. No part of this workbook may be reproduced in any form without the permission of the author. The views expressed in
 this book are not necessarily those of the publisher.

www.abcsofpersonalfinance.com

Introduction

This workbook is designed to help you get the most out of the book, "The ABC's of Personal Finance". Personal finance is personal, which means it is different for every single person. This workbook will help you take the knowledge from the book and apply it specifically to your life and finances.

Make sure that all of your answers are honest and truthful, even if it hurts. Being honest about your situation and your thinking will help you to reach all of your financial goals and dreams.

My hope for you is that by the end of this workbook, you will have the beginning of a great plan for your life and you will have identify some positive changes you can make to get the most out of your finances.

Doing nothing will never move you forward. Go get 'em!

A is for Attitude

A positive attitude is a major key to your financial success. You need to be honest about your current attitude in order to see if any part of it is holding you back from achieving your financial goals.

Is your glass half empty or half full? _____

List your positive attitudes: _____
_____
_____

List your negative attitudes: _____
_____
_____

Are you a goodfinder? _____
- ❖ Do you look only for the good in others and affirm them? _____
- ❖ Do you look only for the good in each situation? _____
- ❖ Do you see the blessings in the problems? _____
- ❖ Do you know that there is a rainbow after every storm? _____
- ❖ Do you look at the good in yourself? _____
    - o Name 3 good things about yourself: _____
    _____

- ❖ Do you look at the good in others? _____
    - o Name 3 good things about your spouse, kids, or friend: ____
    _____

- ❖ Do you look at the good in life? _____
    - o Name 3 good things in your life right now: _____
    _____

Do you have a Wilderness Mentality? _____
- ❖ Check any of the following situations that apply to your currently:
    - o Your future is based on your past and present circumstances. _____
    - o Someone else is responsible for your mess. _____
    - o You make the easy decision whenever you can. _____
    - o You complain every time you see something you don't agree with. _____
    - o You want everything as soon as you want it. _____
    - o Your attitude and behavior is not your fault. _____
    - o You don't deserve for anything bad to happen to you. _____
    - o You want something that someone else has already. _____

If you checked anything above, what changes in your attitude do you want to make? _____
_____
_____

Make the following sayings a part of your everyday life:
- ❖ My past is my past, it is over. My future is not here yet. I can only control today and today is going to be a great day.
- ❖ I am responsible for my mess and I am also responsible for fixing it. I am going to write my own story and it is going to be great.
- ❖ I am willing to take the hard road now in order to have it easy later. The easy way isn't always the best way.
- ❖ I will stop complaining. It doesn't add anything positive to my life.
- ❖ I am willing to wait. I don't have to have everything right now.
- ❖ I am in control of my behavior and I can be anyone I want to be.
- ❖ I deserve great things to happen to me. When they don't, that is okay. I will always make it through.
- ❖ I am going to live my life, not someone else's.

B is for Buying a House

The top American dream is to own a house. That house should be a blessing and not a nightmare. First, make sure you are ready financially and then make sure you buy the house of your dreams within your budget.

1. How much debt do I (we) need to pay off in order to prepare to buy a house? _____
   How long will this take (approximately)? _____

2. How much is six to eight times of my (our) expenses, what we need in an emergency fund? _____
   How long will this take (approximately)? _____

3. What is 25% of my (our) take home pay per month? _____
   This amount will be the most we can afford in a monthly mortgage, including insurance and taxes.

4. Based on the answer in Question 3, what is the maximum mortgage we can afford (again including insurance and taxes)? (Use any mortgage calculator to determine this amount. Do not rely on the bank to tell you this information.) _____

5. What is 20% of the amount in Question 4? _____
   This is the amount you will need to save as a down payment for your house. Any less will cause you to have an additional payment for PMI. How long will this take (approximately)? _____

6. Based on Questions 1-5, how long (approximately) will it take for me (us) to be financially ready to purchase a house? _____

What can I (we) do to save extra money during this time to speed up the process? What sacrifices are we willing to make for our dream?
_____
_____
_____

Do any of the following scenarios apply to me (us)?
- ❖ Someone in the household is in the military _____
- ❖ We have been married less than 2 years _____
- ❖ There is a job change happening or in the near horizon _____
- ❖ I have gone through a divorce in the past year _____
- ❖ I have lost my spouse in the past year _____

If any of the above scenarios apply to you or you are saving for your new house, you will want to rent for at least a year or until you reach your goals.

Buying a house is a long time commitment and you need to take your time to find a great house. You don't want to settle, you want to find something that you will be happy in for at least 10 years.

Do you love the location? _____
        the layout? _____
        the lot? _____

These things you cannot change. Remember, you can change colors, cleanliness, and condition. These items are important, but can be changed.

C is for Cash

One of the biggest tools to help you with your spending is to use cash (literally) for everything that you can. And the only way to move forward is to only buy something if you literally have the cash.

What would your household budget look like if it was a cash only budget? Using the example from page 38, write out your budget, omitting all debt. How much cash would you have left over every year using a cash only budget? _____

What line items on your budget can you use the envelope system for?
_____
_____
_____
_____

Take this time to set up envelopes for the following items:
- ❖ Groceries
- ❖ Eating Out
- ❖ Clothing
- ❖ Mad Money
- ❖ G.O.K. (God Only Knows)
- ❖ Medicine
- ❖ Gas
- ❖ Auto Expenses
- ❖ Gifts

...and any other items listed above that you need.

Make a list of everything that you use your credit cards for and make the decision to use cash or debit cards instead. Write out beside each item on your list whether you are going to use cash or debit card. If you are using a debit card, write out the conditions of the purchase. For example, you use your credit card to rent a car. Beside this item, write down to use your debit card instead and then write down that you will need $100 extra at the time of rental and that it will be returned as soon as the car is returned.

How much cash do you have in your emergency fund currently (available for immediate use if necessary)? _____

How much cash do you want in your starter emergency fund (if you do not have an emergency already)? _____

How fast can you reach this amount? _____

Debt will never move your forward. In fact, you will never be wealthy with debt. Using cash and having cash is the biggest key to not using debt.

D is for Debt

Walk in your truth!

List all of your debts. Remember, a debt is anything you owe. Period. Make sure you include your student loans and your mortgage. Write out the name of the company, type of debt, monthly payment and balance.

What is your total debt? _____
Remember, you can't fix your issues if you are not honest with yourself.

In what order do you want to pay off your debts? Remember, do what is best for you and will motivate you forward. _____

What sacrifices are you willing to make to pay off your debts? (example: take on a second job or turn off cable) _____
_____
_____
_____

Do you need to do any of the following to help you clear debts?
- ❖ Sell your car with a payment and buy a car with cash
- ❖ Sell your house with a mortgage and rent until you are out of debt
- ❖ Sell a collection such as stamp, car, jewelry, etc.
- ❖ Sell stuff on eBay or Craig's List

Considering all of your resources, how long do you think it will take you to get out of debt not including your mortgage? _____
Including your mortgage? _____

How many of the debts on your list are collection debts? _____

List them out, smallest to largest, and use these steps to settle any collection debts (to be done after current debts are paid off):

1. Start with the smallest debt. Gather enough cash together to offer around 10 – 15% of the total debt.
2. Contact the collection company and make them an offer as a "settlement in full". They probably will not accept the offer the first time. Call about once every couple of weeks and keep making the offer to settle.
3. When they accept the offer, make sure to get the offer in writing, either mail or email, before you send them the money and make sure it is a "settlement in full". Once you receive the deal in writing, send them a cashiers check or money order. NEVER GIVE THEM ACCESS TO YOUR BANK ACCOUNT INFORMATION.
4. Staple a copy of the payment to the settlement letter and keep in a file, forever. Odds are it will come up again and you will need proof that you settled the debt.
5. Follow the steps above to pay off all of your collection debts. If you are having trouble with one company, you can skip them and move on to the next one and come back to them.

You can settle past debts yourself. Do not let collection companies bully you or scare you into paying them before you can. They cannot threaten you and if they do, just hang up. You may owe the debt, but you don't have to be bullied into paying.

E is for Excuses and Expectations

Excuses and wrong expectations are nothing but obstacles to get in your way and prevent you from having everything you want to have.

What are some of the excuses you are using right now when it comes to your money and your debt? (Be honest) _____
_____
_____
_____
_____
_____

What recent purchase or purchases have you justified, either to yourself or someone else? _____
_____

Why did you feel like you needed to justify the purchase? (For example, was it because you didn't have the money to pay for it or you really didn't need it?) _____
_____
_____

If you are not where you want to be financially, who do you (honestly) believe is responsible? Who do you blame? _____
_____

Why are they to blame? What did they do to cause your problem? _____
_____
_____

What are your expectations when it comes to your finances? _____
_____
_____

Based on your current finances, do you expect to have a great future, a mediocre future, or a bad future? _____

What can you do to change any mediocre or bad expectations you have to great expectations? _____
_____
_____

After reading the book, what are your realistic expectations for your finances for the next 3 years? _____
_____
_____

For the next 5 years? _____
_____
_____

Remove your excuses and make your expectations great and realistic and you will have a great life.

F is for Financial Checkups

What are your bank fees per account per month? _____
_____

How much does it add up to each year? _____

Do you have overdraft protection on your account? _____
How much do you spend in NSF fees per year? _____

How much does your bank charge if you do not use their ATM? _____

List any other fees your bank charges, even if just once a year, and write down the total for the year. _____

TOTAL BANK FEES PER YEAR _____

Do you have health insurance through your company? _____
If not, use an independent insurance agent to find a plan you can afford.

Do you have a whole life insurance policy? _____
How much do you pay per month for this policy? _____

Do you have a term life insurance policy? _____
How much do you pay per month for this policy? _____

According to your independent insurance agent, how much would a term life policy be for you at ten times your income for 15-20 years? _____
_____

How much would you save per year by switching from a whole life policy to a term life policy? _____

What is the deductible for your auto insurance policy? _____
What is your yearly policy amount currently? _____
What would your yearly policy amount be if you changed your deductibles to $1000? _____
How much savings per year would this change provide? _____

Do you have a will, power of attorney, and living will? _____
Make sure that all of your legacy papers and anything that your family will need is all in one place.

How much of a tax refund do you get back every year? _____
Divide this amount by 12 and how much are you overpaying to the IRS every month? _____
Using the withholding calculator at www.irs.gov, what should my new withholding be? _____ Put this on a new W-4 and give to your payroll department.

Make sure that you are performing a financial checkup in all areas every 6 months. Make sure you are always looking for the best coverage at the best prices.

G is for Guardrails

What are your current guardrails in the following areas:

Debt _____
_____
_____

Time _____
_____
_____

Spending _____
_____
_____

Savings _____
_____
_____

Giving _____
_____
_____

What are some new guardrails you want to establish in the following areas:

Debt _____
_____
_____

Time _____
_____
_____

Spending _____
_____
_____

Savings _____
_____
_____

Giving _____
_____
_____

List each activity you kids are involved in, the cost of each activity, and the time it takes per week for each activity: _____
_____
_____
_____
_____

How much do you spend in gas for these activities? _____
How much do you spend in eating out for these activities? _____

What activities can be eliminated or done in a different way in order to free up money and time with your family? _____
_____
_____

What percentage of your take home pay are you currently:
    Spending _____
    Saving _____
    Giving _____

What categories need to be adjusted in order to follow the "secret" of 80-10-10? _____
_____

H is for Habits

What are your good habits? _____
_____
_____
_____

What are your bad habits? _____
_____
_____
_____

List each bad habit and put a cost to it, per year. Be honest about the actual cost by using your spending journals, bank statements, etc.

Do you have any addictions? If yes, please list and place a cost beside each one. _____
_____
_____
_____
_____

How many traffic violations have you had in the past 3 years? _____
How much did these cost you in fines, insurance, etc? _____

What habits do you have that you believe, if changed, would save you money? _____
_____

How much do you think it will save you per year? _____
_____

Please circle which habits below you believe you have most of the time:

Patience	Impatience
Saver	Spender
Cash	Debt
Think	Impulse
Discipline	Undisciplined
Wisdom	Society
Giving	Selfish
Peace	Stress
Freedom	Pleasing Others
Learn from your mistakes	Keep making same mistakes
Humble	Haughty
Kindness	Anger
Satisfied	Keeping up with the Joneses
God's Way	Man's Way

If you circled any on the right, what steps can you take to reach the ones on the left? _____
_____
_____
_____
_____
_____

Don't let your bad habits keep you from reaching your dreams.

I is for Ignorance, Indulgence and Impatience

What areas of personal finance and your money are you ignorant in (remember ignorant means without knowledge, not stupid)? _____
_____
_____
_____
_____

What can you do to gain more knowledge in the areas above? _____
_____
_____
_____

Who can you talk to as a mentor in the area of money? _____
_____

What bill(s) are you ignoring right now because you are scared of the result? _____
What steps can you take to overcome this fear? _____
_____

What are some indulgences in your life? _____
_____

What are you buying or participating in currently that you can not afford? _____
_____
_____

How can you have these items in a way that you can afford (ex: paying for a college education)? _____
_____
_____

How can you correct an indulgence you already participated in (ex: sell a car)? _____
_____
_____

How much money did you spend this week out of impatience? _____
_____
_____

How much debt to you owe due to impatience? _____
_____
_____

What steps can you put in place to overcome impatience when making financial decisions? _____
_____
_____
_____

Remove the 3 I's from your life in order to reach your dreams!

J is for the Joneses

Who are your Joneses? _____
_____
_____

Do you believe that you are trying to keep up with them out of jealousy or discontentment? Or for some other reason? _____
_____

What are you jealous of? What do you wish you could have that someone else you know has? _____
_____
_____

What do you have that someone you know is jealous of? _____
_____

Would you be willing to give them that item? _____

What steps can you take to be happy with or without your "stuff"? _____
_____
_____
_____

Do you own the stuff you own because you truly enjoy it or are you trying to be someone you are not? _____

Are you content enough to not buy anything new for a month or even a year? _____

Can you be happy where you are right now for a year? _____

If you see someone else getting something new, especially something you want, can you be happy for them? _____

Say goodbye to your Joneses and be content with what you have and what you can afford.

K is for Kids and Money

From whom are your kids getting their education regarding money? _____
_____

What are you teaching your kids about money? _____
_____
_____
_____

List your kids, their ages, and what information for each kid you should be giving them at this time. _____
_____
_____
_____
_____
_____
_____
_____
_____
_____

When your kids are ready for college, how will you help them to find their passion? _____
_____
_____
_____

What steps are you and your kids going to take to pay for college without debt? _____
_____
_____
_____
_____

Have your kids ever asked you to lend them money or cosign for them?
_____

If you said yes, did it hurt your relationship? _____

What steps can you take to put the relationship back where it should be? (ex: forgive the debt and move on) _____
_____
_____
_____

Are you enabling your kids to continue in bad financial behavior? _____
_____

What changes can you make in order to end the enabling? _____
_____
_____

Love your kids enough to say no. Love your kids enough to teach them. Love your kids.

L is for Life and Legacy

What does your current snapshot look like? How much life insurance to you have? How much retirement do you have? Do you have the proper legacy papers: a will, a power of attorney, and a living will? _____
_____
_____
_____
_____
_____
_____
_____
_____
_____
_____
_____
_____

Check off what is in your legacy drawer or book:
- ❖ Life insurance policies _____
- ❖ All bank account information _____
- ❖ All retirement accounts information _____
- ❖ A copy of your will _____
- ❖ A copy of your power of attorney _____
- ❖ All mortgage information _____
- ❖ A list of all of your debts _____
- ❖ Social security information _____
- ❖ The contact names of your lawyer, accountant, financial advisor and executor of your will _____

- ❖ A list of your funeral information and wishes _____
- ❖ A list of all of your usernames and passwords _____
- ❖ Deeds for all property _____

What is your legacy? What will you be remembered for when you pass on? _____
_____
_____
_____

What do you want to change about your legacy? _____
_____
_____
_____

Be the best you you can be and leave the legacy you want to leave.

M is for Marriage and Money

Do you and your spouse work on money issues together? _____

Do you make all financial decisions together? _____

Do you and your spouse do a monthly budget? _____

If not, why? _____

_____

Do you and your spouse fight about money? _____

If so, what are the main issues? Why do you fight? _____

_____

_____

Do all of your bank accounts have both of your names on them? _____

If not, why are you or your spouse keeping a separate account just for you? _____

_____

Is there anything you own that you feel like is just yours, not your spouse's? _____

Why are you unwilling to share this item? _____

_____

Have you ever committed financial infidelity, even once? _____

If so, what was the item and why did you feel the need to keep the purchase from your spouse? _____

_____

_____

_____

_____

_____

Do you know your spouse's story? If so, please write it out. If not, list some questions you can ask them in order to make them feel comfortable about sharing their story with you. _____

_____
_____
_____
_____
_____
_____
_____
_____

What can you and your spouse do better in the area of loving and respecting each other?

Love	Respect

Marriage is about love and respect and being a team. Remember, there is no I in team.

N is for Need vs. Want

How much do you spend each year on your needs (shelter, utilities, clothes, food, and transportation)? _____
_____

Where can you save money when it comes to your needs? _____
_____
_____

How much do you spend each year on your wants (everything not listed above including your debt)? _____
_____

Where can you save money when it comes to your wants? _____
_____
_____

Are you working in your passion? _____
Are you working to pay for your needs or your wants? _____
What wants can you eliminate and begin to go after your passion? _____
_____
_____
_____

What in your life, your stuff, are you not satisfied with? _____
_____
_____
_____
_____

What are you looking to upgrade before it needs replacing? _____
_____
_____

What is your true reason for upgrading it? _____
_____
_____

What steps can you take to change from an upgrader to a replacer? ____
_____
_____
_____
_____

Know your needs from your wants. You can have both, but make sure your needs are covered first.

O is for Out of Balance

Do you feel like your finances are in balance between working, spending, saving, and giving? _____

If not, what do you feel like is out of balance? _____
_____

What steps can you take to place the items above in balance? _____
_____
_____
_____
_____
_____
_____

What is your reference point, your goal? _____
_____
_____

What are some constant corrections that you should be looking out for when it comes to your personal finances? _____
_____
_____
_____

What are your objectives for the next 5 years? _____
_____
_____

What have you sown recently that has brought you a bad harvest? _____
_____

Why did it reap a bad harvest (go wrong with consequences)? _____
_____
_____

What have you sown recently that has brought you a good harvest? ____
_____

Why did it reap a good harvest (go well with good results)? _____
_____
_____

What lessons can you learn from the bad and the good harvest to reap great harvests going forward? _____
_____
_____
_____

Are you a good or bad money manager?
_____

What changes can you make to become a great money manager? _____
_____
_____
_____

Live a balanced life!

P is for Perspective

What would your perspective of the letter in the book be if your child sent it to you? _____
_____

What is your perspective of your personal finances? _____
_____

List all of the good things about your finances: _____
_____
_____
_____
_____

List all of the bad things about your finances: _____
_____
_____
_____
_____

For every bad thing listed above, what step can be taken to make it good?
_____
_____
_____
_____

What do your worry about when it comes to your finances? _____
_____
_____

What can you change in order to relieve the worry? _____
_____
_____
_____

What is a financial challenge you are currently facing? _____
_____

Treating your challenge as a puzzle, identify the following steps: _____
- ❖ Lay out your pieces _____
_____
- ❖ Establish your borders _____
_____
- ❖ Don't force a piece that doesn't fit _____
_____
- ❖ Do a little at a time _____
_____

Always keep a positive outlook when it comes to your money. Adjust your perspective accordingly.

Q is for Questions

What is your:

Why? _____
_____
_____
_____
_____
_____
_____
_____
_____

What? _____
_____
_____
_____
_____
_____
_____
_____
_____

When? _____

_____

_____

_____

_____

_____

Where? _____

_____

_____

_____

_____

_____

_____

_____

Who? _____

_____

_____

_____

_____

_____

_____

_____

_____

_____

R is for Road to Recovery

What do you feel like your biggest problem is when it comes to your finances? _____
_____

Do you feel like you have a ...
- ❖ Discipline Problem _____
_____
- ❖ Entitlement Problem _____
_____
- ❖ Greed Problem _____
_____
- ❖ Coward Problem _____
_____

What steps can you take to fix any of these problems in your finances? _
_____
_____
_____

What changes in your personal finances can you make in order to change your household finances (excluding the government and others as an answer)? _____
_____
_____
_____
_____

_____
_____
Who are you blaming for your situation? _____
_____
_____

What are some solutions for your situation? _____
_____
_____
_____
_____

Start your road to recovery now!

S is for Spending Plan

Are you currently doing a monthly spending plan? _____

What are your reasons for not doing one? _____
_____
_____

Are you willing to start doing a spending plan immediately? _____

If not, what are your reasons? _____
_____

Are you currently keeping a spending journal? _____

If not, what are your reasons? _____
_____

Are you willing to start a spending journal immediately? _____

How much money can you save per month by doing a spending journal and spending plan? _____

List some immediate savings you can find in your spending plan:
_____
_____
_____
_____
_____
_____
_____
_____

Spending Plan Worksheet

2a. Fixed expenses

Housing
- Rent or Mortgage $_____
- Insurance/Taxes* $_____

Utilities
- Telephone $_____
- Heating $_____
- Electricity $_____
- Trash/garbage $_____
- Water $_____
- Sewer $_____
- Cable $_____
- Other: _____ $_____

Credit Card Payments
- _____ $_____
- _____ $_____
- _____ $_____

Auto
- Loan payment $_____
- Insurance* $_____
- License $_____

Child Support/Alimony $_____

Life Insurance* $_____

Other
- _____ $_____
- _____ $_____
- _____ $_____

Total Monthly Estimated Fixed Expenses $_____

2b. Controllable expenses

Food
- Groceries $_____
- Food eaten out $_____

Household Expenses
- Repairs & supplies $_____
- Furnishings & appliances $_____
- Outside upkeep $_____

Transportation
- Gas and repairs $_____
- Other transportation $_____
  $_____

Personal/Medical Care $_____

Education/Reading $_____

Travel & Entertainment $_____

Child/Elder Care $_____

Charity/Gifts/Special Expenses $_____

Clothing $_____

Savings $_____

Other $_____

Total Monthly Estimated Fixed Expenses $_____

* Monthly portion of premiums if NOT paid by employer OR automatically deducted from your paycheck OR listed with your periodic expenses on page 2.

Reproduced with the permission of Michigan State University Cooperative Extension

T is for the Ten Commandments of Personal Finance

How do you fare with each commandment and what can you change about each one?

I. Thou shalt not use debt and credit cards. _____
_____
_____

II. Thou shalt only have a mortgage if the payment is less than 25% of your income and is on a 15 year fixed rate and you put at least 20% down. _____
_____
_____

III. Thou shalt never co-sign or lend money to a friend or family member. _____
_____
_____

IV. Thou shalt always pay with cash. _____
_____
_____

V. Thou shalt always budget and treat that budget like a contract. _
_____
_____
_____

VI.   Thou shalt always have an emergency fund. _____
_____
_____

VII. Thou shalt save for retirement. _____
_____
_____

VIII. Thou shalt give. _____
_____
_____

IX.   Thou shalt always have integrity. _____
_____
_____

X.   Thou shalt always have hope. _____
_____
_____

If you follow these ten commandments, you will always have success.

U is for Unique

What things do you do that are considered normal? _____

_____
_____
_____
_____
_____
_____
_____
_____
_____
_____

What things do you do that are considered unique? _____

_____
_____
_____
_____
_____
_____
_____
_____
_____
_____
_____
_____

What changes can you make in your finances to become a unique person, not normal? _____
_____
_____
_____
_____
_____
_____
_____
_____

V is for Vision

How do you view your past? _____
_____
_____

How do you view your present? _____
_____
_____

How do you view your future? _____
_____
_____

Knowing what you know now, what would you change in your hindsight?
_____
_____
_____
_____

What are you focusing on today? _____
_____
_____
_____
_____

What is your vision for tomorrow? _____
_____
_____
_____

What are your visionary money goals? _____
_____
_____
_____
_____
_____

What obstacles are in the way of these goals? _____
_____
_____
_____
_____
_____

Never give up on your dreams or visions.

W is for Wisdom

What is a major financial decision you are making or have made recently? _____
_____

What are the consequences of this decision in 10 minutes? _____
_____
_____

What are the consequences of this decision in 10 months? _____
_____
_____

What are the consequences of this decision in 10 years? _____
_____
_____

Are you a critical thinker or do you go along with everyone else? _____
_____

If you are not a critical thinker, what is stopping you? _____
_____
_____

Have you made any recent financial decisions based on feelings instead of common sense? _____
_____
_____
_____

If so, what was the result of these decisions? _____
_____
_____
_____

What would the result have been if you had used common sense instead of feelings? _____
_____
_____
_____

X is for X-Ray

Please answer all of the questions in the book.

What about you, on the inside, would you change? _____
_____
_____
_____

What about you, on the inside, do you believe is holding you back? _____
_____
_____
_____

Y is for You

You are the answer. Why do you believe you are the answer? _____
_____
_____
_____

What are you doing that will move you and this country forward? _____
_____
_____
_____

What is your story? Write out what you want your story, going forward, to look like. _____
_____
_____
_____
_____
_____
_____
_____
_____
_____
_____
_____
_____

What lifestyle changes can you make to be successful financially? _____
_____
_____
_____

What feelings do you have that are getting in the way of your financial success? _____
_____
_____
_____
_____

Who do you want to be and how can you get there? _____
_____
_____
_____

Z is for Zoie Lovell King

Who is the person in your life that you most admire? _____
_____
_____

What attributes of this person do you admire most? _____
_____
_____

How can you incorporate these attributes into your life? _____
_____
_____

What things would you be willing to take from each stop and incorporate them into your life?

- ❖ First Stop 1920 – 1930 _____
  _____
  _____
  _____

- ❖ Second Stop 1950 – 1960 _____
  _____
  _____
  _____

- ❖ Third Stop 1980 – 1990 _____
  _____
  _____
  _____

❖ Final Stop – Today _____
_____
_____
_____

What are your solutions for your future? _____
_____
_____
_____

www.ingramcontent.com/pod-product-compliance
Lightning Source LLC
Chambersburg PA
CBHW081347180526
45171CB00006B/616